Magic in the Garden
Whimsical Adult Coloring Book

By Lilt Kids Coloring Books
Illustrated by Anastasiia Nikitina
liltkids.com

COLOR TEST PAGE

COLOR TEST PAGE

"Enjoy free bonus images from some of our best-loved coloring books on the next few pages."

Find our books on Amazon.

IN MY ENGLISH GARDEN
Beautiful Illustrations For Adults Color

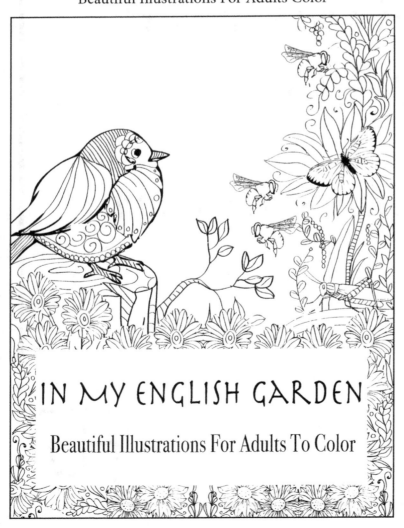

OCEAN FANTASY
Beautiful Mermaid Coloring Book For Adults & Children

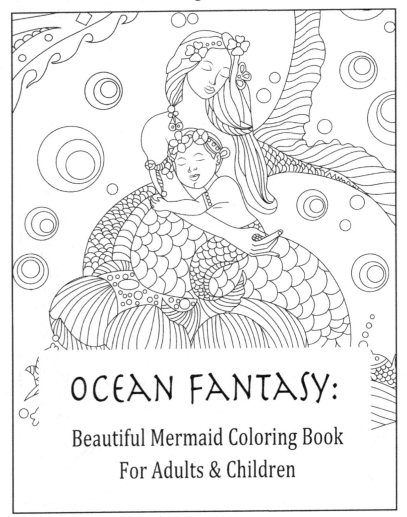

OCEAN FANTASY:

Beautiful Mermaid Coloring Book
For Adults & Children

MAGIC OCEAN ADVERNTURE
Adult Coloring Book

Magical Ocean Adventure

Adult Coloring Book

COLORING INSPIRATIONAL QUOTES
The Uplifting Coloring Book For Adults

Every day is a good day

Coloring Inspirational Quotes:

The Uplifting Coloring Book For Adults

Like us on **f** facebook

Are you an Adult who Likes to Color?

You've got friends!

Meet others who love to Color just like you in our online community.

Share your work or see what others are coloring.

Free coloring book giveaways!

Go to LiltKids.com and join our Facebook group or email list. Or search Facebook, Twitter, or Pinterest for "Lilt Kids".

Made in the USA
Coppell, TX
19 June 2020